For John Briggs

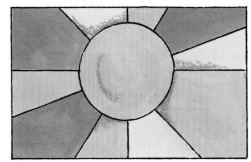

Special thanks to the
National Weather Service in
Burlington, Vermont

Library of Congress Cataloging-in-Publication Data

Gibbons, Gail.
Weather words and what they mean / by Gail Gibbons.
p.   cm.
Summary: Introduces basic weather terms and concepts.
ISBN 0-8234-0805-1
1. Weather—Terminology—Juvenile literature.
2. Meteorology—Terminology—Juvenile literature.
[1. Weather—Terminology.
2. Meteorology—Terminology.]
I. Title.   QC981.3.G53   1990
551.6′014—dc20   89-39515   CIP   AC
ISBN 0-8234-0805-1
ISBN 0-8234-0952-X (pbk.)

ISBN-13: 978-0-8234-0805-4 (hardcover)
ISBN-13: 978-0-8234-0952-5 (paperback)

ISBN-10: 0-8234-0805-1 (hardcover)
ISBN-10: 0-8234-0952-X (paperback)

The weather changes from day to day. Weather words explain what the weather is like outside.

AIR PRESSURE

High pressure is when air particles are close together. The air is usually cool and dry. High pressure often brings fair weather.

LOW PRESSURE

Low pressure is when the air particles are farther apart. The air is usually warm and moist. Low pressure often brings bad weather.

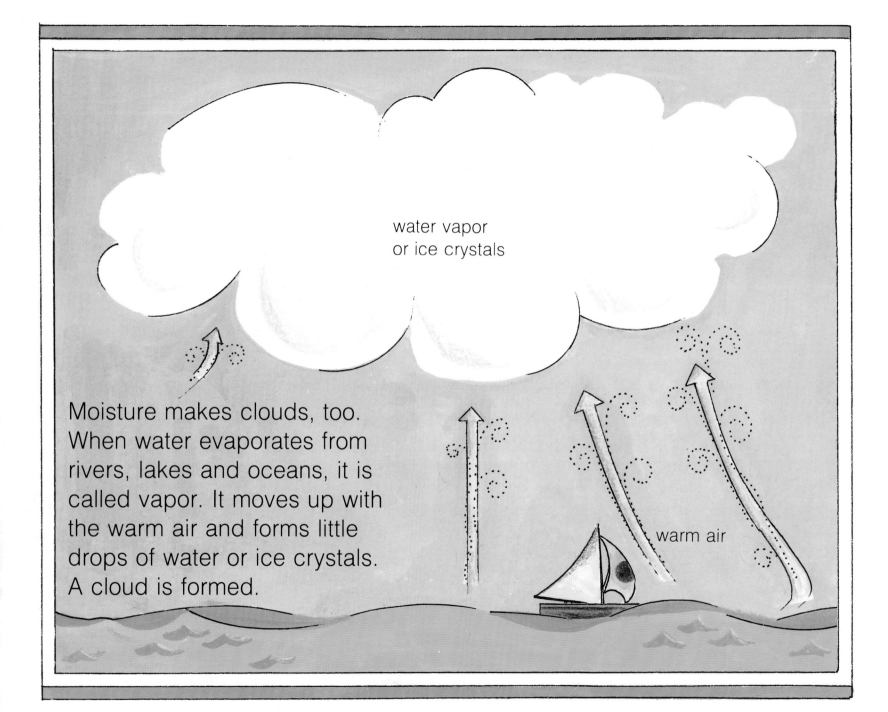

water vapor
or ice crystals

warm air

Moisture makes clouds, too. When water evaporates from rivers, lakes and oceans, it is called vapor. It moves up with the warm air and forms little drops of water or ice crystals. A cloud is formed.

Clouds come in all shapes and sizes. There are three main kinds of clouds.

Cumulus clouds are puffy. They are fair weather clouds.

PARTLY SUNNY

PARTLY CLOUDY

Cirrus clouds are the highest clouds. They mean fair weather, too.

CLOUDY

Stratus clouds are low, gray clouds. Sometimes, they bring rain or snow.

There are other kinds of clouds with long names. They are combinations of cumulus, cirrus and stratus clouds.

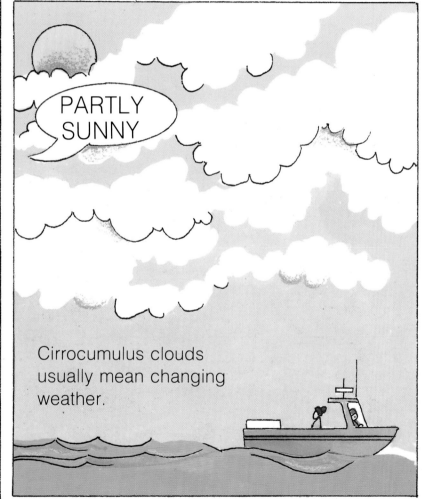

PARTLY SUNNY

Cirrocumulus clouds usually mean changing weather.

Cirrostratus clouds often bring rain or snow.

CLOUDY

Nimbostratus clouds bring rain or snow.

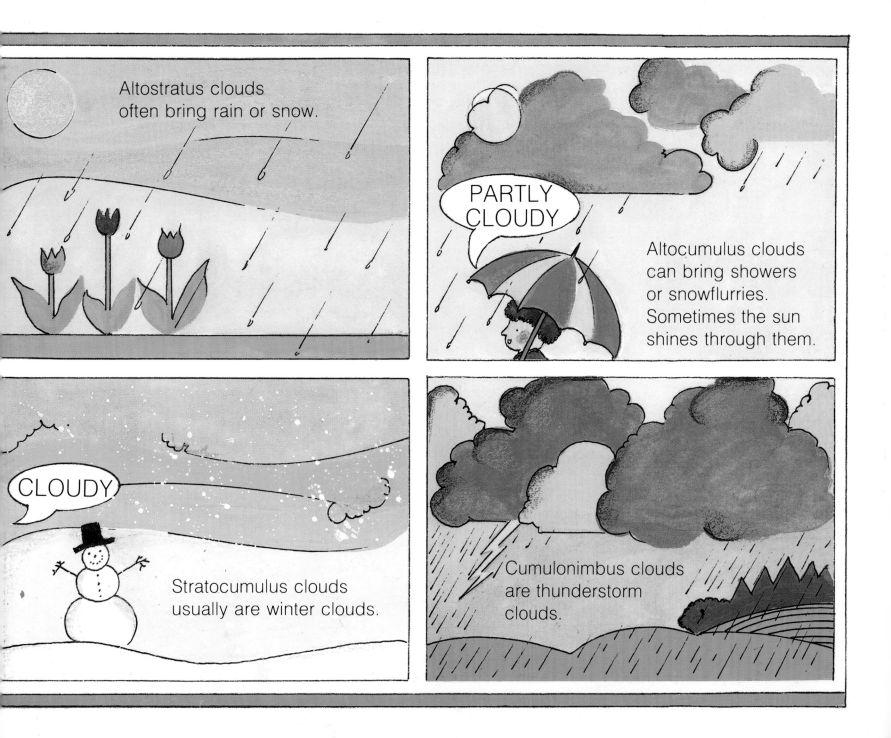

A cloud close to the earth's surface is called fog.

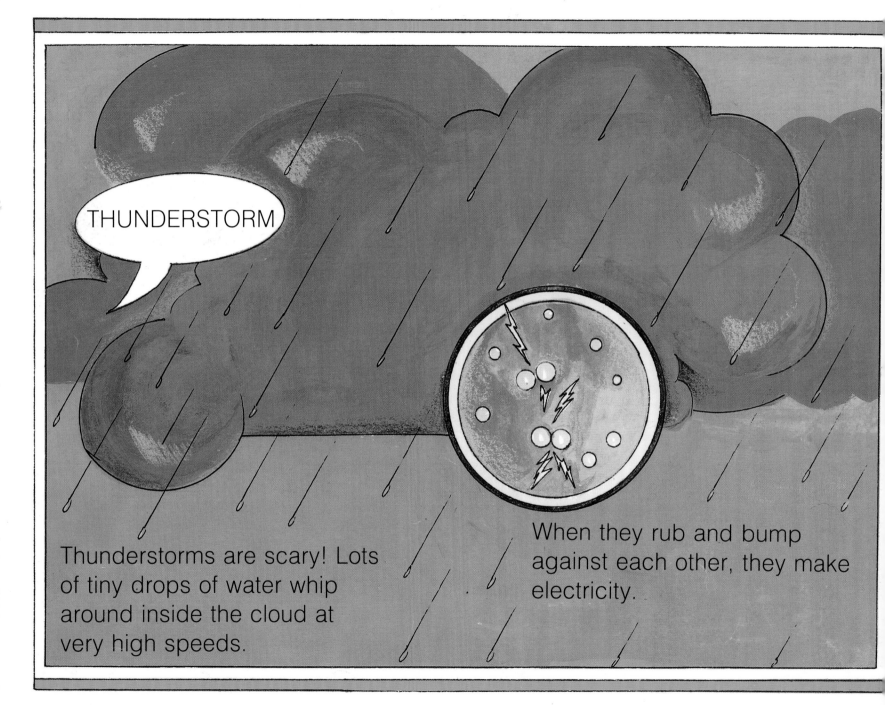

THUNDERSTORM

Thunderstorms are scary! Lots of tiny drops of water whip around inside the cloud at very high speeds.

When they rub and bump against each other, they make electricity.

When enough electricity builds up, it bursts through the cloud and flashes. This is called lightning. Lightning is very hot. It heats the air around it. The hot air expands and . . . BOOM! It makes a loud noise called thunder.

THUNDER

LIGHTNING

RAINBOW

Everyone loves looking at a rainbow! This may happen while it is raining, or just after the rain stops. When sunbeams shine through drops of rain, the light breaks up into seven colors. A rainbow appears.

Sometimes in the winter it snows. Snow crystals form when water freezes inside the clouds.

When the snow crystals join together, they become snowflakes.

When they are heavy enough, they fall.

SNOW

HAIL

Sometimes it hails. Inside the cloud ice crystals are tossed up and down. Water vapor freezes onto the ice crystals in layers. When they become heavy enough, they fall as hailstones.

WIND

Wind happens when warm air moves up and cooler air moves in to replace it. Warm and cool temperatures affect the wind speed and direction. Wind direction is where the wind comes from.

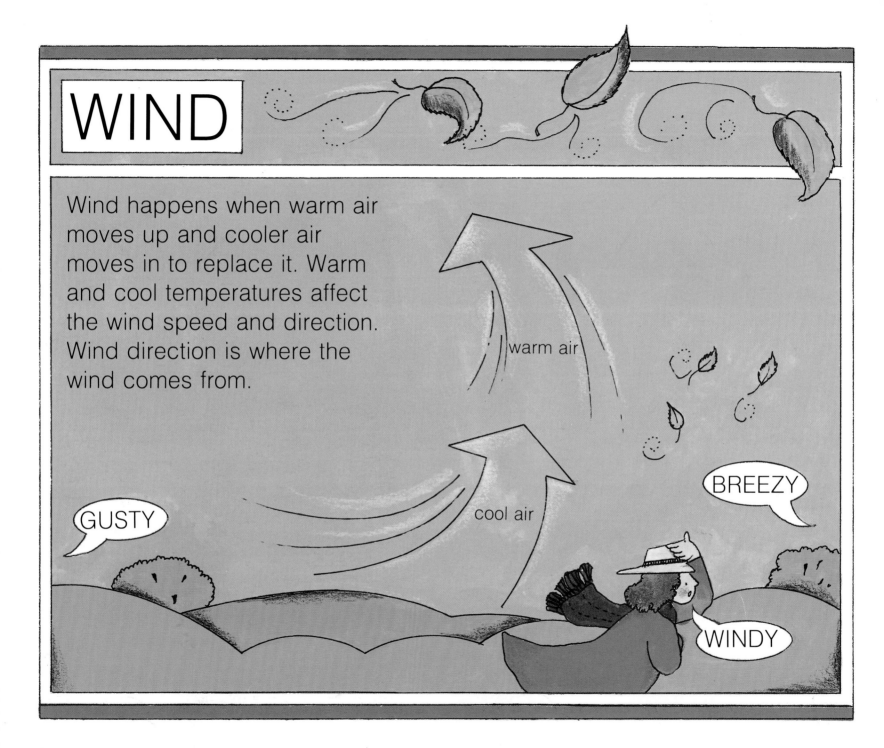

When wind blows with more and more force, a windstorm develops. There are many kinds of windstorms. Often, they cause damage.

A hurricane is a spiral-shaped windstorm that comes from the tropics.

HURRICANE

A tornado is a funnel-shaped windstorm that twists as hot air spins upward.

TORNADO

A gale is a strong windstorm.

GALE

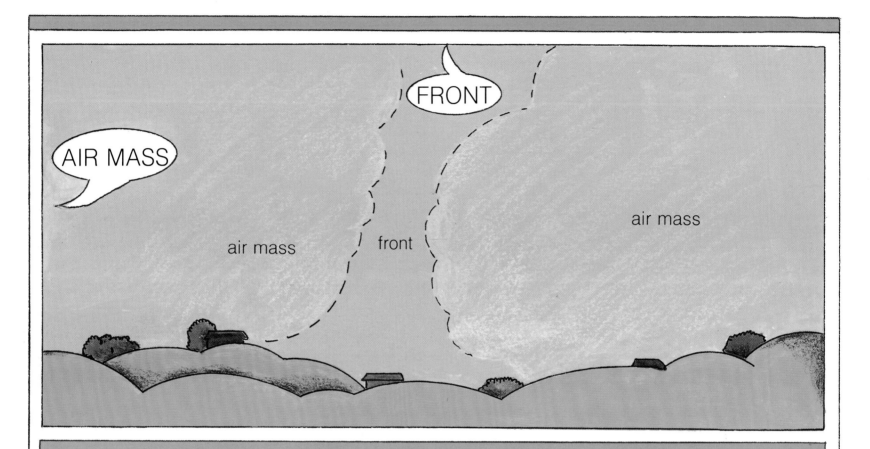

The many combinations of temperature, air pressure, moisture and wind create different kinds of weather conditions. A big area of weather that is the same is called an air mass. The boundary between two air masses is called a front. This boundary is where the weather changes.

The weather is hardly ever the same from day to day.
That's why it is so interesting.

The driest place in the world is a desert in Chile. It hasn't rained there for over 400 years.

A number of years ago in France, a tornado crossed a pond and sucked up everything. At the place where the tornado stopped, the people had a surprise rainfall of fish and frogs!

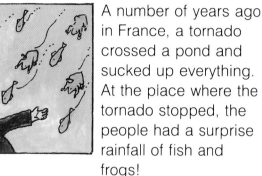
There is enough electricity in one flash of lightning to light a house for one year.

It rains more days each year on Kauai, Hawaii than in any other place in the world. There it rains about 350 days a year.

The coldest recorded temperature was in Antarctica. It was −126° Fahrenheit (−88° Centigrade).

The hottest recorded temperature was in Northern Africa. It was 136° Fahrenheit (58° Centigrade).

Sound travels at 1088 feet per second. If you are one mile from lightning, it will take about five seconds for the sound of thunder to reach you.

It's believed that no two snowflakes are ever the same.

The highest wind speed ever *recorded* was 231 miles per hour in 1934 on Mt. Washington in New Hampshire.

REMEMBER . . .
When you hear a weather forecast that gives storm warnings, pay attention. Be careful.